ASTRO-WINGED DESIRES

ASTRO-WINGED DESIRES

by
David A. Farsang

NORTHWOOD INSTITUTE PRESS
Midland, Michigan 48640

First Edition

© 1981 by Northwood Institute Press

LCN 81-80732   ISBN 0-87359-025-2

Printed in the United States of America

DEDICATION

I humbly dedicate this book:

to Kathy and Barbara, my wife and daughter respectively, for having faith in me; to Margaret, who speaks the most eloquent Queen's English of which some (hopefully) was rubbed off on me; to Marjorie, for giving me renewed inspiration; to Lona and Bea, for their valued friendship; to Parm Mayer, for his bequest of the magical palette of multicolored phrases and metaphors; to artists Susan Stair Stevens and Katharine S. Pettigrew whose graceful works add much to the book; to Kathy, an English major, who upon reading my "Will I Still Be Waiting When Aurora Calls . . .?" (sent to her parents, Johann and Arthur Turner) remarked that; "It is really very good." To all of these, and others who thus supplied the much needed encouragement which eventually led to this publication.

I also dedicate this book to love that constantly fills my heart, as it regenerates as fast as I am afforded a chance of sharing it with others.

But most of all, I dedicate this book to my adopted Country, The United States of America, for giving me a taste of true liberty which is now an integral part of me; for which I would gladly give my life if called upon.

The great Hungarian poet Sándor Petőfi, expressed it with unequaled eloquence:

"Liberty and love—these two I need to have.
For love I would gladly sacrifice my life;
for liberty I would sacrifice my love."

And now, to further expose a divested soul which is beyond aspergill cleansing.

David A. Farsang

CONTENTS & TITLE INDEX

Snow In Vermont 1
. . . It Seemed As If I Had a Choice 2
Will I Still Be Waiting When
      Aurora Calls . . .? 4
A Sonnet From the Eastcoast of Barbados 5
Northbound On Astro-Dreams 6
On a Sunny Day, I Opened My Window 10
RFD 4, Box 281 11
Dear Lillian: 12
Parm Mayer, a Constant Teacher, a Poet 13
Wildflowers 14
A Sonnet to a Friend 15
Twentieth Anniversary of a Twentieth
      Century Messiah 1959-1979 17
Excelcius 19
The First Spring 20
Terpsichorian 21
Conversation with a Silent Friend 22
Encomium to Martin Luther King .23
A Sonnet From Redkill Creek 24
A Supplication 25
Jamaica, Where I Almost Found Paradise 26
The Ultimate Reward 28
A Végső Jutalom 29
A Legacy 30
Omega 31
Bricks of Love 32
An Invocation . . . .
For Newlyweds: A seven point philosophy
      for lasting happiness 34
Light Verse
      Diogenes' Lantern 36
      Information, Please 36
      When Snowflakes Fall 36
      Happy Birthday! 36
      Six Months Paid Vacation (Twice a Year) 37
      Spring 37
      From Ebbetts Field 37
Angry Ocean 38
Silence 38
Pygmalion 39

One More Rubicon 39
A Sonnet From Harpswell's Shore 40
Christmas Messages:
     Three Little Words 41
     A Christmas Vision from Maine 41
     Resurrection of the Soul 41
Philosophical Thoughts 42
     Spring Without Flowers 43
     No Longer Nadir, Not Yet Zenith 43
     Specious 43
     Bosom-Prisoned Love Is: 43
     Rearview Mirror 44
     Vertex 44
Anne 45
A Misnomer 46
. . . Long Have Ended the Race 48
John's Island Reverie 49
A Eulogy 50
Illusion 51
The Last Ion 52
A Spring For All Seasons 53
Homo Sapiens 54
To the Mother of My Child 57
An Apparition 58
Somewherebound 59
A Sonnet to Span an Ocean 60
Impetuous Youth 62
Leda 66
Love Is 67
Dulcis Vitae 68
A Vermont Winter Through a Frosted Window 70

FOREWORD

Writing poetry can be painful. It can be a heart-pounding and soul-baring experience. Exposing one's innermost thoughts to a critical public takes great courage with expectation that at least some readers will understand the abstract images drawn in this black and white shorthand.

Poetry is, at best, a shorthand device to structure the framework of ideas, allowing the reader's imagination to fill in the gaps; to flesh out the complete thought.

David Farsang writes beautiful poetry; abstract, full of analogies and similes; thought provoking and stimulating. I find that after reading his words I think to myself; "I wish I could have said it that way."

So read the words and let your mind-image soar without bounds. The endless discovery of truths will make the reading of this book all the more enjoyable.

Alfred M. Worden
1981

Colonel Alfred M. Worden is the former astronaut and pilot of Apollo 15. He is also author of "Hello Earth," a book of poetry, relating to his trip to the Moon, aboard the Space Ship Endeavour.

SNOW IN VERMONT

A gigantic world carpet with greed,
decadence and sufferings swept under it,
to be disgorged by the ravaged earth
to feed the fledglings.

An often wiped slate that held many
never-to-be-fulfilled promises.
Underneath, dormant embers,
half-surrendered dreams of frustrated,
but not defeated youth.

A soft cuddly shroud to cushion the
bludgeonings of want, to gild the
specious pledges so copiously given
by worldly diplomats — in the tongues of Babel.

Haughty in short lived omniscence,
each onrushing spring unearths new decays,
stunted earthy growths when crocuses
popping to freedom, when the robins come . . .

Surely, last winter's inadequacies.

Surely, this alfa-green spring through
an omega-red fall will cleanse our
oft-crusaded world, alleviate the
miseries . . . hush the frantic cries.

But then, winter returns,
and snow falls in Vermont
once again . . .

K.S.P.

1

. . . IT SEEMED AS IF I HAD A CHOICE

From echoes
of long suppressed desires
Leda appeared with honeysuckle lips;
tantalizing, pink-nippled breasts
firm and heaving seductively
with every undulating stride,
like an epode set to music by Apollo.

Tyndareus forsaken . . .
a moral breach, an unspanable chasm,
deep and as wide as eternity
between heaven and hell.

Could I have
gone either way . . .?
For a fleeting moment,
it seemed as if I had a choice.

If I succumbed,
could I glide over the raging,
sky-lapping inferno on swan's wings?
Could I reach the prelude to imagined
heavenly bliss, before the feathers
go up in flame . . .?

If I do not
chance it, will I ever find
the fantasized fulfillment?

. . .Denuded bones
will not regenerate the flesh that
became viand for the vultures of time;
extreme poverty of the soul.

The seeming
choice was only a mirage . . .
I have crossed my Rubicon,
and locked the door to Elysium eons ago.
Key defiantly flung away . . .
pulp devoured together with the sinew
that moved once flesh covered bones
hellbound.

S.S.S.

3

WILL I STILL BE WAITING WHEN AURORA CALLS . . .?

Treading on crimpy, yellowed leaves,
Casting elongated, looming shadows . . .
Lambent beneath a mercurial sky,
In search of an ephemeral Spring
That comes between Summer and Fall . . .

Once fertile wet-green hills, now blanketed
With footprint-destitute crackling snow . . .
Hard, and black under the white disguise,
. . . Like unharvested Summer-fruits
Turned insipid on unreachable boughs . . .

To touch the quivering flesh . . . be skin-to-skin
With Spring that bursts magnolias in bloom.
. . . Thwarted by unyielding bones . . . pulsating red marrow
Taps-out unspoken promises to slake the hunger,
Or be consumed by the holocaust within . . .

But the rainbow-lure is flame to the moth-heart;
Wearily, the relentless search goes on,
Bypassing blossoms made fertile by Summer bees . . .
Much like countless, gray yesterdays
That vanished into the night . . . without a trace . . .

This poem was sent to Johann and Arthur Turner. See reference to it in my dedication.

A SONNET FROM THE EASTCOAST OF BARBADOS

This ultra-love came not from a mother.
    This love began and ended in a sigh
    Uncherished, unfulfilled—destined to die.
This love is most unlike any other.
This love could have brought delight and laughter,
    But tearless eyes could neither laugh nor cry.
    Fragrance of friendly Trade Wind hovered high
Over sunken waves of grave disaster,
    While the unhealed wounds of bygone passion
Concealed behind an esoteric gaze.
    Ultimately, every false confession
Will be lost in Life's mysterious maze.
    The murmur of the white-crested ocean
Bade The Bearded One to divest the haze.

NORTHBOUND ON ASTRO-DREAMS

A titanic arrow shot through the air,
I know (?) how far will it travel . . . and where.

   Exhilarated by
the thrill of soaring above clouds, with mind
ebullient—it was a champagne flight.

   Bubbly nectar
poured by some goddess from Mount Olympus
with ebon hair, doe-topaz eyes and wine enamored
crimson lips . . . fully spread eagle's wings
pinned onto her sky-blue lapel. I closed my eyes
for a short wink of millenniums . . . Zeus embodying
her idol, seducing her in cozy, willing embrace;
her naked, ethereal from snuggling against the
dark side of my divested soul . . . Gurgingly,
she brim-filled my glass anew with floating
Bacchic delight.

   Thoughts cruising
at 37,000 feet above popping-cotton-field clouds . . .
non-Avian feathers, crimpy autumn leaves,
destined to the whims of irresulute winds in the
vastness of an overbearing, orderly universe.

   To amuse myself,
I was playing a fascinating game, matching clouds
against their chimerical shadows reflected on the
green-velvet ocean below when an air-current,
no doubt commended by irate gods, shook me from
my fantasized world . . . Encaged in unpenetrable
nebulae, unyielding sea of pernicius miasma
exuded from prejudiced, overrested minds.

S.S.S.

The limitless
horizon drew from me a fathomless sigh, reminding
me of what liberty once was . . .

In this physical
proximity to God, somehow the distance between us
seemed to be greater. In the past, when I felt
closer to Him, I was farther away.

At the vanishing
point where infinity began, specks of billowing
white-dots—seeds of mundane escapades of the
soul-destitute flesh— were bobbing in and out
of sight.

Life, fragile
and thought-provoking as birth and rebirth . . .
without it, there could be no future for Death.

Somehow, I was
not a stranger in this heavenly kingdom, although
I could never be one of its citizens . . . I would
not abase the last vestige of my soul with
adulation, nor would I succumb to hypocrisy.

Will the
Ultimate Flight be like this . . . will I be
colliding with shooting stars . . . or other
floundering souls . . .?

A buzzing
in my ears gave evidence to our sudden descent . . .
a roller coaster leaving its apex lightning fast,
with illusions and fragments of dreams left beyond.
Pine-spired land rising to meet us in a dark,
cynical welcome . . . will it all end in bone-crushing,
marrow-spilling disaster . . .?

A sharply
etched vision from mnemonic depths . . . desolate,
atom bomb-scarred field strewn with charred
bodies—claimed by no one. Vulture stripped
ribs and worm-hollowed fibulae protruding from
once fertile earth, remnants of long forgotten,
"I told you so . . ." prophets.

ON A SUNNY DAY, I OPENED MY WINDOW

I opened my window to let the sunshine in . . .

Faintly, I heard Irene's timid entreaty, and in
olive-poor Eden white doves took to wing.

Then, tormented butterfly-tranquillity descended
on blooms of blushing meadows in their springtime
gaudiness.

Weary, sunken-faced slouching figures marching by . . .
time-soiled venerable hands clutching the hands
of yet unlived children . . . humming a wordless, familiar
threnody. Others leaning heavily on brotherhood-crutches;
sinking deeper and deeper into timeless, fickle sand.

Were they searching for unrestrained shepherd stars,
unlike the Crescent Moon, the Stars of David and
Bethlehem, with their seasonal limitations? The three,
at times, nearly touching in the deceptive sky,
yet many light-years apart on this ravaged earth.

Was it just a shimmering mirage through pearled-up
tears, a vision of peace on earth that someday might
become reality . . .?

With chagrin I realized what had taken place:

I opened the window to let the sunshine in . . .
and a dream escaped . . .

RFD 4, BOX 281

In the delta of a nameless rill and the Green River
That became turgid and turbulent from the spring thaw,
Stands a welcome-faced red and white house.
The house is peopled with laughing children,
Hopefilled youngsters, a variety of cats
And a pitch-black puppy dog.
The parents radiate contentment and understanding
As they listen to the myriad of questions
Hurled at them by the ever-inquisitive children,
Who are playing with the ursine puppy.
The seemingly unconcerned cats keep their eyes
Resignedly on the rustic bird feeder,
Where song-destitute woodpeckers gorging on suet,
Thoughtfully provided for them
At the front of this peaceful house of yesteryear.
. . . And as if suspended in time, there are no harsh
Sounds to be heard in this Shangri-La . . .
The churning of the river, a stammering proclamation
Of an ever-so ephemeral tranquillity.

DEAR LILLIAN:

One of my early English teachers introduced me to poetry and to three poets in particular. They were the "established" William Ernest Henley and Robert Frost, and a relatively unknown poet, Parm Mayer.

I admired Henley for his then daring views as far as the British Press was concerned. Frost I accepted as the "Vermont Farmer of Rhymes," down-to-earth, with a hoe in one hand and a pen in the other. They were good, but woefully conventional, adhering to boundaries dictated to them by artless bureaucrats.

In Parm Mayer, I found the skilled smith of phrases and metaphors . . . an artist who painted vivid pictures with words.

I understand him better than all the others I have ever read in English . . . I was greatly influenced by him . . .

All of us who knew Parm Mayer personally or through his poetry—miss him, but consoled by the knowledge, that he left us in the corporeal sense only. His infinite wisdom lives on . . . his poetry remains a constant inspiration . . . a gushing fountain of Hippochrene . . .

I humbly dedicate the enclosed poem to Parm's memory and deeply regret that I have met him only through his poetry . . . I would like you to share these feelings with me . . .

Lillian Mayer is the widow of Parm.

PARM MAYER, A CONSTANT TEACHER . . . A POET

Pegasus borne . . . on swift wings of yearning
sored to escape earthy limitations,
to appease a constant quest for learning,
to ridicule gilded imitations.

Hippochrene's waters nurtured his thurst
to guide and impart knowledge to mankind.
A teacher of truth, but a poet first:
His wisdom lives to weed the fuzzy mind.

WILDFLOWERS

A meadow, my soul's
Innermost reflection,
Vivid and craving for
    Tenderness and bliss.

To be adored, but
Not with mere compassion.
To adore and tremble
    While consumed by a kiss.

A SONNET TO A FRIEND

Fiftieth year . . . the sun is bright and high;
The Future is teeming with fulfillment.
The Past in a gossamer confinement
And there's not a cloud in the azure sky.

In retrospect of the decades gone by
There is a stimulating element;
The years did not diminish your confidence
In that infinite love you glorify.

Though you never backed away from a fight,
With diplomacy, averted combat.

The Road you chose is harsh and recondite,
Still you advocate love, not tit-for-tat.

For you strangers never appear in sight,
Only future friends you have not yet met.

For Arthur Turner, January 30, 1981.

S.S.S.

TWENTIETH ANNIVERSARY OF A TWENTIETH CENTURY MESSIAH 1959-1979

As a child, in my fantasized world, I asked a magnificent leopard in a well-kept zoo;

"Are you happy here, where you need not hunt for food or compete for territory? Where your star-studded beauty is displayed for thousands, where you impart joy to all the children just by pacing back and forth in your well equipped clean cage?"

The splendid beast stopped as if startled, and for the first time I have noticed the raw flesh of his shoulders. His unseeing eyes penetrated the thick stone walls . . . and beyond.

"The stars give joy in their infinite freedom . . ."

The faraway growl might have been a resignation. Blood oozing from the shoulder wounds, continued the hopeless pacing, rubbing against the rough steel bars with every turn.

Many years later while roaming the countryside I admired a majestic mountain. Its snow-capped peak piercing the sky, reaching beyond the wildest imagination of my searching heart. And yet, I was unable to accept it as the ultimate freedom.

The immobile mountain is but a slave to the earth. Callous feet trample and disfigure its mighty bulk while obdurate miners tunnel into its regimented, docile rocks to spill the contents of its maw.

Then, a vigilante of the sky, an eagle on the wing caught my eyes. The earth engulfed me in a spiraling wild furry and all at once, freedom BECAME!

I knew then, that freedom must be available to all, that all must have the right to harvest and savor the fruits of their labors, utilize their talents and initiatives, that freedom is indeed, worth fighting for.

The leaders of our beloved country have wavered, gone astray from the austere road of righteousness, from our God-charted fateful destination.

Our proudly billowing tattered flag that was honored at Fort McHenry and moon-planted by intrepid astronauts, now desecrated by misguided patriots.

We were in dire need of a redeemer, a staunch standard-bearer of our cherished principles—the need was urgent.

To answer the call, in nineteen-hundred-fifty-nine, a coterie of dedicated few with vision, love for liberty and a firm belief in the American Free Enterprise System, founded Northwood Institute.

The Herculean infant, born into modest circumstances, developed rapidly under steadfast guidance with the aid of a few devoted patrons. Now, a fomidable youth of twenty with thousands of noble benefactors, Northwood endeavors to accomplish the Eurysthean tasks of NOW.

Northwood with its living green campuses, devoted administrators and teachers is indeed, the advocator and expounder of the free enterprise system—the basis and backbone of our democratic society.

Northwood's foretold possibilities HAVE exploded, penetrated the limitless horizon like a space ship from Cape Canaveral, shrinking the unknown, kicking open tightly shut doors of ignorance. Northwood's guiding light spreads irresistably to nourish the innovative mind—to free the darkness-slave.

In a typical Northwood-state-of-mind, I quote from John Philpot Curran:

"The condition upon which God hath given liberty to man, is eternal vigilance."

Northwood is eagle in the sky!

EXCELCIUS

You're all around me!
    The roar of the wounded ocean,
    The cry of graceful gulls,
    The black crag defying the waves,
The crest of bubbling lace.

You're all around me,
    The spires of pine afar,
    The setting sun,
    The breath of Zephyrus
Soothing my face.

You're all around me,
    The moonlit sky,
    The wrathful tempest,
The earth.

You're all around me,
    I'm overjoyed,
I'm hurt . . .

THE FIRST SPRING

Beneath a country lilac bush
laden with redolent blooms,
enamored with spring perfume
a fragile maiden of guileless yesterdays,
became a woman . . . with dreams for tomorrow.

The rapture-fertile swarthy earth
engulfs the fatuous seed,
but there is no guarantee
that the haphazardly fallen acorn
will ever be a stately oak:

There are squirrels
lurking in the countryside . . .

TERPSICHORIAN

A world of castle-in-the-sky, of intricate schemes,
Moon-high leaps through clouds, a knight in shining armor;
    Aegis-arms to snuggle into between dreams.
    Oh, but fantasized reality is far more
        Sweeter when fulfilled,
A touch of autumn-summer—winter not yet chilled.
        The brightest of twinkling stars
        Were plucked by soft and cuddling arms
    Stumbling often while trying.
        Violets thus crushed through rising years
    Could not be silenced by caustic tears
        Nor resurrected by subtle crying.

CONVERSATION WITH A SILENT FRIEND

Troubled and despondent, I was talking to my friend
who listened with great concern,
nodding occasionally, but not of approval.
My friend knew fully well that I did
not seek approval of any kind.
The nods were revelations of cognizance
to the anxieties I was burdened with, an
assurance to help by being so conspicuously silent.
My friend never advised me nor belittled my
apprehension: I am grateful for that.
The onus was heavy and mine alone, and yet,
greatly alleviated when I shared it with my friend.
Thank you for the "I-told-you-so-less" listening;
for not assuming the role of Pygmalion.
Thank you for remaining my friend.

AN ENCOMIUM TO MARTIN LUTHER KING

I do not pray for your soul . . .
        You were as close to the image of our Creator
        As a human being ever hope to be.
The opulance of wisdom you impart
        Will linger in our hearts for ever.

No, I do not pray for your soul,
        But if I may, I will join in your prayer,
        The prayer that I know you pray . . . even now.
Let us pray for the souls of those
        Who defile our societies with hatred;
        Let us pray for the souls of those
Who can rejoice in human sufferings;
Who would deprive others of their birthrights.

Let us pray for the souls of the so-called lawmakers
        Who legalize the assassin's acquisition of firearms.

        But most of all, let us pray for the souls of those,
Who acknowledged with glee the news of your
Tragic and untimely departure . . .

A SONNET FROM REDKILL CREEK

Shielded from the ills of this strife-torn world
Beaneath blue skies at placid Redkill Creed . . .
The tranquil scene would render Ares meek,
    His existence incongruous—absurd.
    In one's mother-tongue praises seldom heard;
Youth with dreams branded indolent and weak.
In Babel's confused tongues our leaders speak
    To hide the betrayed trust—they claim they've earned.
Hackneyed slogans—more unkept promises
    For a tomorrow that may never dawn.
Sanguin, unlived youth with unkissed kisses;
    War-gambit sacrifice . . . mere fallen pawn.
Irene's chance to meet Ares, misses.
    He eyes the eagle; she cuddles the fawn.

K.S.P.

A SUPPLICATION

For your restless heart I wish fulfilled love;
For your perplexed soul, tranquility and peace.
For your searching youth, intrigue and excitement.

For your Fate, I wish for the softest glove;
For your wand'ring mind—the turmoil to cease.
For your yearning body, the hug of contentment.

JAMAICA, WHERE I ALMOST FOUND PARADISE

Could I be indifferent
to the constant wailing of the sea,
to this sleep-destitute lullaby;
this harbinger to usher in the day
that ends the night of undreamed dreams,
      the night of yearned-for ecstasy?

Could I be indifferent
to the myriad of blossoms that beholds the eye
every step of the way;
to the fluttering-jewel butterflies
or to the Doctor Bird's stand-still flight
      beneath the golden sun-spilled sky?

Could I be indifferent
to the stream of children gushing from open-air schools,
to the parched-face drivers of donkey-pulled carts;
to the reapers of sugar cane in carefree siesta
beneath the umbrage of a stately banyan tree
      that blissfully protects and cools?

Could I be indifferent
to the prancing, spring-feverish haughty youth
weighed down with hope and unspent love?
Fantasized dreams not yet drained from their souls,
unaware of deceitful tomorrows, of Janus-faced life,
    its dream shattering truth.

Could I be indifferent
to the capacity to feel and fully comprehend,
to ache with the waves as they sunder on jagged rocks,
to the euphonic delight of meadowlarks on wing,
or to the pangs of spilt-marrow hurt, when a delicate
    orchid is crushed by an indelicate hand?

No, I cannot be indifferent
to the stench of poverty or to the fragrance of acacia,
nor to the vicsissitudes of only dreamed-of fortunes.
I am no stranger to constant green winters;
to the search for caring hands to hold the reins,
    to lead and guide this Eden-Jamaica.

THE ULTIMATE REWARD

You're the Southern Cross that guides me
through onus-laden, sleepless nights and disperse
sunshine at the birth of each dawn.
You're the worshipped idol of my oft-forsaken altar,
    you and your beloved mother.

You're the tranquil haven
in my life's turbulent sea,
the joyous songs of carefree nymphs.
You're the Future, you're Faith, Hope and Charity,
    you and your beloved mother.

You light up the austere road I travel,
allay fear and mollify dejection.
You're my exalted, sacred inspiration,
my constant spring, my ultimate triumph,
    you and your beloved mother.

You will be there to tenderly caress
my silver-templed weathered face
when twilight comes to joyfilled years.
You're more than a privilege to live for,
    you and your beloved mother.

Barbara's birth, translated from the Hungarian.

A VÉGSŐ JUTALOM

Te vagy Dél-csillaga álmatlan éjszakámnak,
S a virradat napfényét Te adád.
Te vagy imádott bálványa oltáromnak,
   Te, és a drága jó anyád.

Te vagy a rév életem viharzó tengerén,
S a Sellők örömdala áriád.
Te vagy a Jövő, a Hit-Remény-Szeretet,
   Te, és a drága jó anyád.

Te vagy világító fáklya élet-utamon,
S csüggedni nem hagy vidám harsonád.
Te vagy a szent cél, a végső diadal,
   Te és a drága jó anyad.

Te vagy ki majd deresedő hajam csókolá,
S aki enyhíti majd életem alkonyát.
Te vagy kiért élni több mint jutalom,
   Te és a drága jó anyád.

Borbála születésére

A LEGACY

For Barbara's Graduation.

I wish for you constant sun-filled Springtime,
Never to suffer Winter's loneliness,
Never to have your love unreturned
And not just a mirage your happiness.

Never to be lost in the turbulent sea,
But in a haven safe and content.
Never to be troubled by unending nights
Nor terrified by ill portent.

Be chary with your memories . . .
Save for tomorrow some precious happy hours.
Beware of the thorns among the roses
—Your tears would only wilt the flowers.

Do not save Life's fruits for distant days.
Unharvested they'd turn insipid and stale.
The heart needs love and must be conquered
And will not break if it should fail.

Sing then with Euterpe's inspiration;
Neither covet nor do others blame.
Life and love has always been mysterious.
. . . No two yesterdays will ever be the same.

OMEGA

On denuded, barren willow branches
    the tempest strums the icy song of Fall,
as I cast the last of Summer-glances
    and heed eternal Winter's muted call.

Ardent lips—once advocates of Summer—
    now fettered beneath everlasting frost.
In pursuit of Life's elusive glamour
    neither was I chary of love—nor cost.

Grant this last request of my tranquil heart,
    let me linger for the final embrace;
let me sort out, let me justly impart
    mementoes of Life—medals of the Race.

The Autumn leaf is no match for the gale.
    I drift along to bournes I do not know.
Mem'ries of past Summers cannot prevail . . .
    I tread on—leave no footprints in the snow.

BRICKS OF LOVE

Basked in tropical Florida sunshine,
reveled in still-falling virgin Vermont snow
and all that laid between oceans were mine
while the moon shone bright, many springs ago.

Summers had gone and winters passed me by,
but the season's most admired wonders
were fickle as the mercurial sky
that prompted my vagabond heart's wanders.

To sip nectar from twinkling buttercups,
to breath in the fragrance of the thistle;
to count the tap-taps of summer raindrops
while list'ning to the northbound train's whistle.

Memories . . . foundations for a future
to build with bricks of love mortared with dreams.
Episodes to cherish and nurture;
be cuddled by the warmth of youthful gleans.

AN INVOCATION

As children by our parents we were told,
"Be true to your friends and respect the old."

In school we heard our teachers emphasize,
"To succeed in life, youth must compromise."

As youngmen, while sowing our wild oats,
pursuing prankish thrills and petticoats,

brainwashed into yokes by decrepit laws;
became war-gambit's nugatory pawns.

Wars have been contrived in plush offices
by rulers with deceitful promises.

They preach water while drinking vintage wine,
grant fallen youth a medal—or a shrine.

Parents must refute "Politician's Truth,"
reverse the tide and learn to respect youth.

. . . Youth can be reckless and magnanimous!
Let us pray for lasting peace—all of us.

FOR NEWLYWEDS:
A seven point philosophy for lasting happiness

1. Aim your goals in life high, but not out of reach. Divide it into many (20 to 25) significant stages.

2. Take a pause after reaching a plateau and reward yourselves with a vacation, or at least with a sumptuous night out.

3. If you should ever quarrel or become discontent with one another (hypothetical of course), recall the day and the days that followed your wedding. Remember how prescious you were to each other? Now smile, kiss and make up!

   No one is ever completely wrong or completely right, not even you.

4. Save 10% of your net earnings, give 10% to charity, and spend every cent of the remaining 80% on yourselves. Never lose sight of the fact, that money has only one function—to better your lives.

   If you fail to do this, you could become slaves to money or enslaved by it.

5. This is the time to begin collecting memories for the future. This is also the time to live for NOW.

   Leave the woes of your tomorrows for the next day when they become todays. With this time-lapse, you can cope with it less impulsively.

6. To get along with the rest of the world (including in-laws), allow five demerits for every merit you could find in others. Many more good points could be found just under the surface. All you need is the willingness to find them.

7. Last, but by no means the least. Remember that all of us have feelings, and that careless words could inflict greater pains than "Sticks and stones . . ." You cannot make a human being inferior by derogatory remarks any more, than make yourself superior by self-proclamation.

   If God would not have wanted us to be different, He could have created all of us alike. And what a calamity that would be!

LIGHT VERSE

Diogenes' Lantern

To find an honest man
was one of Diogenes' many ambitions.
Alas, he never had a chance,
He searched among politicians.

Information, Please

If Mr. Ford would have more often
listened to Mrs. Ford,
he would have been less often
misinformed.

When Snowflakes Fall

People 'round me shiver in
sweaters and fur coats.
I'm warm without any,
wrapped in sexy thoughts.

Happy Birthday!

In stone it should have been carved
onto Moses' monumental page
and advocated by Confucius
the legendary sage.
"Give pearls away and rubies . . ."
But not your rightful age.

Six Months Paid Vacation (Twice a Year)

Overpaid Congressmen
when briefly assembling
recess-studded sessions
that's vaguely resembling
a search for Ways and Means,
to cloak their dissembling.

SPRING

Tall, slender palms sway from the touch
of Zephyrus' hand.
Above, carefree swallows frolicking
on wing.
Sun and Ocean converge on
timeless sand.
Oh God, how beautiful you made
this Spring.

From Ebbetts Field

Could there be anything
as beautiful as springtime,
with outfielders catching
line-drives and flies.

Could there be anything
as thrilling as a home run?
I know only one other;
girls catching their guys.

ANGRY OCEAN

Pound the rocks with anger,
Break into tiny hurtful pearls,
The rocks are strong enough
To withstand weighty whirls.

Pound the rocks in despair,
But your Fate is forever sealed.
Your chosen course is final;
The Future stays unrevealed.

Mighty irate ocean . . .
Curtailed and freedom-destitute!
The austere road you choose
Is paved with fortitude.

SILENCE

Silence is meditation for the soul.
It can be the demure, inaudible yes,
or the most thunderous no.
Silence is to listen to the needs of others,
to acknowledge God's wisdom.
Silence is a reverent awe;
Silence is ineffable
—You break it if you say it.

PYGMALION

You've molded me, my punctilious Pygmalion
Until I became putty in your skillful hands.

You've molded me to be one in a million,
Then abandoned me, for not fitting the trends.

ONE MORE RUBICON . . .

Weary wings, if you
        take me with your final beat
to Mount Elbrus
        there will be no recourse.

This love, although
        begun with life, is incomplete,
and there is still
        one more Rubicon to cross . . .

A SONNET FROM HARPSWELL'S SHORE

    Mesmerized by the murmur of the sea,
Whipped blue face held high against icy wind
To hear the sentence of the past rescind:
    At last, I'm not devoid of ecstasy.
    Yet, with tightly shut eyes I still could see
How lost and naked is the soul . . . how sinned.
The shroud of ignorance icicle-pinned;
    Summer-freed to hide gilded falacy . . .
    Days always pursued by nights in the past,
And murky gloom is harvest-time for knaves.
    A penetrating sun might fill this vast
Horizon, but could it free the darkness-slaves . . .?
    Or, would the ray-hopes disappear as fast
As footprints behind gray, receding waves . . .

                              Maine, 1970

This was published in the "Best-Loved Contemporary Poems", 1979, edited by Eddie-Lou Cole.

CHRISTMAS MESSAGES:

Three Little Words . . .

The teachings of all the doctrines,
The Koran, The Talmud and The Bible
would fill a thousand libraries.

And yet, all of it could be compressed
into three little words:

"Love Thy Neighbor."

A Christmas Vision from Maine

Peace on Earth . . . at least all around us.
Tranquility sceptically travels across
our land, then abruptly stops, turns around
and laughs at us who still believe,
that Peace on Earth will come.

Resurrection of the Soul

If we again hope to become worthy of
The Star of David, the Crescent and The Cross,
we must learn to live with Nature — and ourselves.
Our ills beyond the help of naphta-salves.
To purify the soul from vindictive dross,
forgo greed and hatred — for Universal Love.

PHILOSOPHICAL THOUGHTS

Love is like an investment.

The extent of our own love
will determine the returns.

Unlike an investment, however,
love is constantly fruitful.

*

Logic is not one of God's sciences.

When we share our sorrows
they become smaller.

Yet, if we share our joys
they become greater.

*

To create lasting friendship
we must share confidences.

When we confide in one another,
we reveal segments of our
inner-heart and soul, perhaps
unknown even to ourselves.

Sharing such intimacies
is an infinite bond,
the strongest adhesive
between two persons.

*

Unshared love is loneliness.

Spring Without Flowers

What life would be without love is
what Spring would be without flowers.

We need both to fill our hearts with happiness,
to broaden our smiles with that inner glow.

Our joy is greatest, however,
when we are able to share them.

No Longer Nadir, Not Yet Zenith

. . . And then, the road will again be straight,
austere, but no longer descending.
We learn as we mellow under Life's pressing weight,
that love revealed is never condescending.

Specious

It's a fact that disagreements
could be caused by truths or lies,
but woe seldom is the greatest
with the one who subtly cries.

Bosom-Prisoned Love Is:

A rosebud amid thorns.
        The uncut pages of a
        love story.

Rearview Mirror

Maybe no one's wise enough
to answer all the ifs and whys,
but do we really try to see things
through the other person's eyes?

Vertex

Love is heaven — and hell:
Love is dreams, doubts and questions unanswered.
Fulfilled love is nothing missing.

ANNE

A few short
decades ago a brilliant star appeared on the horizon,
spreading wisdom, and filling many hearts with joy.

As a Nova,
the enlightenment continued, until the final,
soul-liberating flash.

Desolation
of the mind followed, when the door to
Elysium burst open—woefully too soon.

As twilight
descend, I search anew the starlit sky.
. . . There's an eternal hiatus staring at me.

Undropping
tears caressed by the evening breeze, as the
cloak of darkness wraps around my empty heart.

July 20, 1979

45

A MISNOMER
Hurricane Season Jitters

"Hazel's on the way," I heard radio warning,
"Do not leave your home this gloomy Sunday morning."

I thought it was just as well and rolled up my sleaves.
I'll catch up with the housework while the tempest peeves.

I switched on the TV set to gather more news.
Behold, came a blinding flash—it blew the main fuse.

The red-hot pressing iron just burned through my blouse,
Stumbled and fell on my . . . face in the unlit house.

My body bruised and aching, blinded by the smoke . . .
I need a refreshing drink, I must get a coke.

Blundered to the kitchen in my desperation
To find the floor flooded—no refrigeration.

I burst into frantic tears and ran to the car
To get away from here fast, anywhere, but far.

But the car wouldn't start, the battery was dead.
A ticket on the windshield: "Ten dollars" it read.

In panic I trod for help through mud and mire,
Finally on the road—with a blownout tire.

I cried then I laughed, but was it really funny?
I "escaped" from the house without any money.

Left the disabled car . . . stricken with ataxy . . .
"Three ten," the meter ticked in the home-bound taxi.

Through my neighbor's window, again news of ". . . Hagel, (?)
This is Radio Swiss—broadcasting from Basel."

. . . LONG HAVE ENDED THE RACE

I do not yearn for the kisses of giggling debutants,
their naive, "let's find out what it is" embrace.
　　Like a dream, it's all behind me;
it all happened at the start of my first race.

I do not yearn for the kisses of decadent women,
to be pawn in their games of "let's be unfaithful."
　　By now, this is all behind me . . .
invoice rubber-stamped: "Services, paid in full."

I do not yearn for the kisses of promiscuous lips,
of jaded, discontent "everybody's" dames.
　　By now, this too is behind me,
still, I cannot withdraw from the futile games.

I do not yearn for the kisses of tainted Lorelies;
to be enticed to a point of no return.
　　Even this is behind me now,
yet I seek new pits to fall in with each turn.

The kisses I have fantasized come from unpainted lips.
Will our paths ever cross . . . and come face to face?
　　Once the heart becomes obdurate
it is too late—Fate long have ended the race.

K.S.P.

48

JOHN'S ISLAND REVERIE

With U.S. Senator, Larry Pressler in mind.

The waves came in overbearing, orderly fives,
deceptively adorned with myriad bubbly wings like
the famed sandals that brought Mercury to his
least eloquent patronage.

This pentatonic acquiesce—disrupted only by the
strident outcry of a lone, sea eagle—ridiculing
oft-repeated specious promises such as the
nomination-seekers in their childish, wasteful primaries.

There is no purity or rectitude in such actions.

The polititians bending with the draft generated
in sinister lobbies by esoteric winds.

The dissemble is all too transparent and alienating.

The churned-up oil-spill miasma, the decades of
closeted tainted past, reaffirming the wedded kinship
with the somewhat-honest "public servants."

The lugubrious waves kept coming persistently,
tatting tiers of soiled bubbling lace, ruffles
for a near-white hymeneal gown for a near-virgin bride.

Vero Beach, 1980

49

A EULOGY

In memorium of Reverend Ladislaus Harsany.

We deeply mourn your untimely passing.
The hiatus you leave in our hearts
Is as deep as it is wide,
But it is spanned by your eternal love and friendship
And the steadfast devotion to your fane.
We mourn you, yet we are grateful and warm in the heart.
Grateful for the joys and for the wisdom
You have imparted to us all;
Warm in the heart, because of the knowledge
That yours was a rich and rewarding life.
Brotherhood was your nourishment and
The waters of Hippocrene quenched your thirst.
The awe you radiate is ever-encompassing,
The scope of your accomplishments
Reflecting forever, through the mirrors of friendship . . .

*

Published in May, 1968, in the Journal of Masonic Life, Seventh District, Manhattan.

ILLUSION

The gossomer-veiled night has fallen . . .
Orpheus began to strum his magic lyre.
As dreams unfold
I softly hold
The girl of my cryptic desire.

As the stars fade with the sunrise,
The horizon's aglow in Aurora's fire.
Must end the ruse
Or else I lose
The girl of my dreamed-up desire.

THE LAST ION

Congress is in session.
To give good impression
They have a discussion
On "equal" taxation.
More oil concession;
Farm subsidization.
Foreign wealth invasion;
Rich man's tax evasion.
Unchecked price inflation;
Childish pre-election;
Campaign contribution.
False news on recession
And spreading starvation
Cause for aggravation.
Leader's law-rejection,
Watergate-dejection.
Bitter recollection
Reason for vexation.
Wrong-way evolution;
Seeds for revolution.

A SPRING FOR ALL SEASONS

It could only come about
when birds will again
be free to soar and sing,

when angry seas of hatred
be calmed by shadows
of Halcyons on wing.

When Love triumphs over greed;
when a feebled Ares
had his final fling.

When peace becomes reality
and flowers burst in bloom
Aurora smiles. 'Tis Universal Spring.

HOMO SAPIENS

Sonnets from upsilon to omega.

I

Fallowed game, chipped tools out of stone
And the wheel had been discovered.
Language born when words were uttered
And earth now destined for his home.
Gregariously he would roam
To places yet undiscovered,
Learned to swim, although he sputtered.
At night he gazed a starlit dome.
From enchanting Avian scena
New heights, new goals he'd aspire.
Was it epochal an era
When he learned to control fire?
Was he so far, yet so near a
Fulfillment of his desire?

II

What did he seek, was it the truth?
Was it how far he should venture
In his world-shaking adventure
That bore him only bitter fruit?
Maybe in his eager pursuit,
Overlooked a vital feature
That would tame and conquer Nature?
Are there truths that none can dispute . . .?
Left the caves, the trees and burrows;
Moved from huts to thatched houses.
Learned to use the bows and arrows;
Loincloth replaced by trousers.
Yet, his safety further narrows;
Covet others' land, and spouses.

III

Petty conquests became hollow,
Dampened by sad tears of Mothers
Shed for fallen sons and daughters;
Victims of the "other" fellow.
It was a bitter pill to swallow
That his truth was not his brother's
That he was at odds with others.
Ready to repent with sorrow.
"There's reward for good behavior."
A message reached him clear and loud.
The voice of a diff'rent drummer
Electrified a spell-bound crowd.
A new altar . . . a new Savior?
". . . Renounce idols, there's but one God!"

IV

Dreaded witch-doctors forsaken
In exchange of saving the soul
And paradise promised for all!
Frustrated and deeply shaken
Realized he was mistaken
When only few answered the call.
Rival doctrines bade to enthrall
And few chose the road he'd taken.
He was stunned, confounded and hurt
In this Babel of pretentions.
"The meek shall inherit the earth."
"Circumscribe your lusts and passions."
"Civilize and attain your worth;
Bring forth all your good intentions."

V

Social graces thus dictated
To use napkin, spoon, fork and knife;
Abolish harem for one wife.
He is now domesticated
Supremacy decimated.
Constrained by feigned threats of strife,
He's all but surrendered his life:
Could never be vindicated!
Still, defeat he can't acknowledge,
Profound, truer-Truths he must find.
. . . Eureka! It's greater knowledge.
Time marched on and left him behind.
He's now in a super college,
Developing an ultra mind.

VI

Sciences and technology,
Things he now began to fathom
Led him to splitting the atom,
Led him dwell in psychology.
. . . On the wall his own eulogy.
Unaware of reaching bottom,
Defiantly pushed The Button!
. . . Melpomene's sad elegy.
This erudite supreme-primate
Tenacious in his conclusion;
Withstood plagues and adverse climate.
Yet, a misguided conviction
Urged him on, and he arrived at
Holocaustic self-destruction.

AN ODE TO THE MOTHER OF MY CHILD

I love you for being the Mother of my child
. . . I would not have destined it any other way.
The taming of your spirit from the wild
Was never on the order of my day.
Accept haven in my willing embrace,
Don't look upon life as an endless race
You must enter and at all cost—win.
Separation lines are razor's edge thin.
Teeming memory-bank, that is Motherhood,
But it's not the only source of earthly good.
The nest should remain intact and warm,
The fledglings will weather the storm.
We were one—though younger when the day begun—
Together we'll find beauty in the setting sun.
Though Motherhood's the ultimate in life,
I love in you the Mother, because you're my wife.

AN APPARITION

When Sacred Stars will penetrate
New Babel's chaotic maze,

Myriad of jewels would shimmer
Beyond heaven's milky haze.

Twinkling moments of Peace on Earth
Timidly pop into sight,

Like fragile Christmas ornaments
Hung from the Backbone of Night.

SOMEWHEREBOUND . . .

Battle-scarred hero on crutches,
a gnarled, braced up palm
with love-starved, embrace-ready fronds
reaching towards earth;
a haven for a mourning dove
pecking at invisible seeds
as a cynical mockingbird, being aware of my presence,
began to justify its name.

Then a dazzling butterfly appeared,
and, like my divested soul
zigzagged from blossom to blossom,
unsettled, unsure . . .

From immeasurable distances,
travel-weary echoes compelled me to perk-up.

The disinclined, indolent sky
slowly pulling over a blanket
of buttermilk-clouds to alleviate the shivers
that ran through my addicted body.

The fluctuating sounds,
now the honk of wild goose,
now the clatter of butterfly wings . . .
a desperate, last minute fix for my run-down being.

The sounds crystalize . . . lifting me from
mundane existence,
like a somewherebound train's whistle . . .

A SONNET TO SPAN AN OCEAN

This love is constant, unlike the shadow
That follows you in good weather only.
Close your eyes and wish for me when lonely . . .
The warmth that radiates will melt the snow;
When you're content without me—I'll withdraw.
Cherish fortune's precious moments wholly,
Let the sun descend—as it must—slowly;
Storms will abate with silver-lining's glow.
Reach for my hand, not only when you're lost
And frightened in Life's turbulent ocean,
When chilling nights loom with infinite frost.
Lullabies we've sung with sweet emotion,
A fulfillment no trials could exhaust.
. . . Distance could not lessen such devotion.

S.S.S.

IMPETUOUS YOUTH

Like a mortally wounded silvery serpent,
Redkill Creek is writhing pain-laden down the
ancient valley—as if in escape—on timeless,
oft-traveled paths spring after myriad springs.

Turgid and turbulent, the reckless creek is gnawing
at the side of the mountain until the granite
overhang collapses from its own weight
and chokes the path that took eons to carve.
The dispersed waters run amuck in aimless confusion.

The new paths will be numerous and narrow;
ununited they would be mere thirst quenchers
for the parched earth. They must merge to renew
the powerful flow that will carve the mighty
mountains anew.

. . . At eons end, there will be no more lofty mountains
and no more churning creeks . . . only endless,
monotonous plains carpeted with unturbulent waters,
slimy from inactivity.
Cronus devoured his offsprings.

Logic would indicate, that the fate of Homo sapiens
is analogous to these events. The warning is ominous;
a Damoclean sword we should be concerned with,
but choose to ignore.

With the force of a thousand creeks, our youth
hurl themselves against all they deem "obsolete;"
attack Hydra-shielded corruption with Don Quixote's lance,
bypassing the greatest weapon at their disposal;
the sacred privilege to vote.

Arrogantly, in our claim to impede nature's
self-destruction, we contrive devastation so perilous,
that eventually it will destroy the world as we know it.
The weight of the onus is crushing . . . we cower and
bury our erudite heads in hypothetical sand.

Could we hope to forestall the catastrophe?
Let us examine some of our actions and inactions.
We replaced parental guidence with wicked affluence
and failed to castigate the dishonest, so-called
public servants. We abandoned our youth to the mercy
of a corrupt, greedy society, worshipers of the
Golden Calf.

The standards our forefathers established were
austere, at times even back-breaking, but it was
basically honest. They were pleased if we continued
in their footsteps. We push our children to
superfluous heights where they are often
ill at ease, discontent, even embarrassed.

We cling tenaciously to the premise that the water
of the creeks is pure and white only.
How long we intend to keep up the dissemble
and deny the existance of volcanic earth
that might tint the creeks brown, or even black?

Must we remain obdurate and condone the sensless
killings of innocent people—under deceptive slogans?
Need we tolerate, even take part in a world-wide
conspiracy to instigate and continue the slaughter
that often paints the creeks red?

We must subject ourselves to serious soul-searching
before we attempt to give answers, and our answers
must be without finality. The little wisdom we have is
woefully inadequate to advise our fellow men;
to save our doomed environment.

Our claim to authority and social prominence
is predicated on the color of the skin,
on the Race, origin and background, even on gender.
These are some of the ulcers in our faltering society;
some of the targets of our discontent youth.

Alas, the rampaging creek that floods the village
overnight cannot be looked upon as beneficial:
It must not be compared to the ancient Nile.
Youth neither should accept our systems and
philosophies wholly, nor should they reject
them in their entirety.

Although we have razed many structures built by our
forefathers, we left enough of the foundation to build on,
to fulfill projected new requirements.
We did not always erect the right structures
and some of our best efforts took dishonest detours
when fallen into unscrupulous hands.

Youth must experiment with methods of their own;
they must have feasible programs and plans.
Without them, they would destroy the very foundation
of social, moral and educational standards that
made their revolutions possible.

Today's youth is not different; only younger
and less inhibited. Nor do the prophets of today
defer to those of yesterday.
Ponder the slogans and philosophies of your leaders.
Weigh carefully what they claim to be;
what they claim others are.

Many of our "public figures" became unduly opulent;
their preachings now, at best, a grotesque farce.
Honest leaders are hard to find, even harder to keep.
Advise your representatives of your needs, of your
hopes, of your dreams. Select them with great care.
Do not squander your precious vote and never
surrender to the falacy that your vote does not count.

It is your inalienable right to receive as much
as you earn and you are entitled to the opportunity
to earn to your capabilities and efforts.
However, you have no right to any
that has been earned by others.

Remember also, that by the time you have tried,
tested and put your plans in operation, the next
generation will be rapping on your doors,
claiming to be misunderstood;
claiming to be mistreated.

But then, you, the impetuous youth of yesterday
will have to supply the answers.

LEDA

Whisper-soft zephyr breezed in; conformed to
the contours of my yearning body in
    a once-in-a-lifetime embrace.

Tears of joy welled from the depths of her eyes.
. . . I kissed away the sweet nectar that glowed
    a nimbus 'round her lovely face.

Fulfilled beyond the fortitude of flesh;
already laden with more delight than
    my tormented heart could endure,

when butterflies flew over smiling daisies
and a philomel called—rendering me
    helpless against Fate's conjour.

LOVE IS . . .

Love is limitless joy;
Love can ache and destroy.
Love is the culmination of hope;
A weighty, fettering rope.
Love is fulfillment of welled-up desire;
Love is agonizing purgatory fire.

    Love is heavenly music
    Played on the strings
    Of pulsating hearts;
    Love is despair-magic,
    The years without springs,
    The venom-tipped darts.

Love is the soft whisper of Erato;
A deserted, crowdless Rialto.
Love is heaven on earth;
Love is Prometheus' hurt.

DULCIS VITAE

Life began on a fulfillment-promising
carefree sunny morning.

Its only vicissitude was
Mother gently pushing me on the swing.

It was obvious by midday
when basketball and tennis came,

that Life was a greedy competition;
no longer a children's game.

As the day wore on, shower-clouds
disrupted my mundane life;

a soulless Faust cheated out of wisdom,
heeded Diana's seductive fife.

By evening, repeated calls for The Hunt
exhausted my capricious heart,

yet, instead of ending some old affairs,
a new one I would start.

Complacent voids were quickly filled
with ego-pleasing platitude

and I continued with my
"live for today, devil-may-care" attitude.

Twilight lured me with denuded laughter
(the frantic tears I chose to ignore).

Splendor beclouded reality;
I paid no attention to the score.

Night-orgy found me in wild embrace,
enamored by Bacchus' sweet wine

and an oft-posessed soulless substance—
much like my own—united with mine.

Midnight delirium tremens:
A skeleton-god stood before the blazing sun;

through flesh divested ribs,
prison-striped the Scourge of God, The Hun.

Dawn alone shared my empty bed . . . the clamor
of bone-striking-bone ebbed away.

My tear-soaked pillow disparaged a Janus-faced Life,
betrayer of a bygone sunny day.

A Vermont Winter Through a Frosted Window

The snow-crested bird feeder was barely visible through
The intricate featherings of the window.
Tiny, frisky feather-balls chick-a-deed their thanks
For the thoughtfully provided suet and bird seed.
Then a trio of white-breasted nuthatches chased them away.
The carefree, upside-down nuthatches were gorging the suet
Until a foursome of juncos put them to flight;
When a pair of phoebes arrived, the juncos fled.
Finally, the quarrelsome, tyrannical blue jays came
And forced the phoebes to abandon the feeder.
There were no reprisals, no follow-ups to these petty conquests.
Ironically, the phoebes and blue jays of Homo sapiens pursue
Their chickadees, nuthatches and juncos and divest them
Of everything. In the wake lies emaciated, bruised bodies,
Bludgeoned into submission by the brute force of
Physical and spiritual deprivation.
The omnipotent super-birds gloat with sadistic glee . . .
The whimpers of hunger merely enbolden them to take more
The drama I have witnessed seemed inherent to nature,
Even poetic, through the icy panes.
With chagrin I curled into the softness of the cuddling chair.
The ephemeral protestations seemed flagrantly incongruous
From the cozy, warm side of the frosted window . . .